PRAISE FOR

HEART OF AN ATHLETE®
PLAYBOOK

Athletics can be a great way to learn lessons about everyday life. But what is really special is when you can take athletic lessons and apply them to your spiritual life. *Heart of an Athlete® Playbook* takes a look at how the tests we face as players and coaches can help us grow as Christians.

Coach Tony Dungy
Former Head Coach, Indianapolis Colts

Staying close to God through the study of His Word is an essential part of any Christian's life. The devotions in *Heart of an Athlete® Playbook* will help you dig into the Word and be encouraged not only in your faith but also in your sport.

Betsy King
Member, LPGA Tour Hall of Fame

Heart of an Athlete® Playbook is a training manual with an eternal goal. Being an athlete, I realize the importance of training and preparing my body so that it is ready for competition. This book will help you train so that you can live life the way God intended.

Chris Klein
Former Midfielder, Los Angeles Galaxy

HEART OF AN ATHLETE® PLAYBOOK

FELLOWSHIP OF
CHRISTIAN ATHLETES

HEART
OF AN
ATHLETE®
PLAYBOOK

DAILY DEVOTIONS FOR
PEAK PERFORMANCE

Revell
a division of Baker Publishing Group
Grand Rapids, Michigan

© 2012 Fellowship of Christian Athletes

Published by Revell
a division of Baker Publishing Group
PO Box 6287, Grand Rapids, MI 49516-6287
www.revellbooks.com

Revell edition published 2014
ISBN 978-0-8007-2506-8

Previously published by Regal Books

Printed in the United States of America

The Library of Congress has cataloged the original edition as follows:
Heart of an athlete playbook : daily devotions for peak performance / Fellowship of Christian Athletes.
        p. cm.
    Includes bibliographical references and index.
    ISBN 978-0-8307-6420-4 (trade paper : alk. paper)
    1. Athletes—Prayers and devotions. I. Fellowship of Christian Athletes.
BV4596.A8H34 2012
242′.68—dc23   2012015007

All Scripture quotations, unless otherwise noted, are taken from the Holman Christian Standard Bible, copyright 1999, 2000, 2002, 2003 by Holman Bible Publishers. Used by permission.

Scripture quotations labeled The Message are from The Message by Eugene H. Peterson, copyright © 1993, 1994, 1995, 2000, 2001, 2002. Used by permission of NavPress Publishing Group. All rights reserved.

Scripture quotations labeled NIV are from the Holy Bible, New International Version®. NIV®. Copyright © 1973, 1978, 1984 by Biblica, Inc.™ Used by permission of Zondervan. All rights reserved worldwide. www.zondervan.com

17   18   19   20   21   8   7   6   5   4   3

Contents

Dear Teammate,

Being on a team—any kind of team—is all about relationships. Whether it's a fellow athlete, a friend or a family member, the only way to truly know a person is to spend time with him or her. These 31 devotionals are designed to help you develop a consistent, focused way of spending time with God. They are written from a competitor's point of view and include Bible verses to help you understand God's perspective on key issues. Our hope is that this book will motivate you to deepen your relationship with Jesus Christ and your understanding of God's Word.

As an athlete, you have been given a tremendous platform from which to influence others. We pray that God will use these devotions to transform your life as a competitor so that you can make an eternal impact for Jesus Christ.

Your Teammate in Christ,

Les Steckel
FCA President/CEO

Training Time

In sports, time-outs give athletes and coaches a chance to strategize for upcoming challenges. Similarly, in life, we need to take time-outs to think about our purpose as members of God's team. FCA is excited to present you with a collection of devotions that will challenge you to play and live for the glory of God. Each devotion is written from an athletic perspective and will encourage you to be more like Christ both on and off the field.

Every morning, set aside a special quiet time to be with God. During this spiritual training time, talk to God and let Him speak to you through the Bible. There are many effective methods that can be used for your daily time with God. One method that we recommend is the PRESS method.

The PRESS Method

Pray

Begin your quiet time by thanking God for the new day, and then ask Him to help you learn from what you're about to read. Prepare yourself by:

- clearing your mind and being quiet before the Lord

- asking God to settle your heart

- listening to worship music to prepare your spirit

- asking God to give you a teachable heart

Read

Begin with the 31 devotionals provided in this book. Also, try reading a chapter of Proverbs every day (there are 31 chapters in the book of Proverbs, which makes it ideal for daily reading), one psalm and/or a chapter out of the Old or New Testament. You may consider beginning with one of the Gospels (Matthew, Mark, Luke or John), or one of the shorter letters, such as Ephesians or James.

Examine

Ask yourself the following questions with regard to the passage you read:

- *Teaching:* What do I need to *know* about God, myself and others?

- *Rebuking:* What do I need to *stop* doing—sins, habits or selfish patterns?

- *Correcting:* What do I need to *change* in my thoughts, attitudes or actions?

- *Training:* What do I need to *do* in obedience to God's leading?

Summarize

Do one of the following:

- Discover what the passage reveals about God and His character, what it says or promises about you, and what it says or promises about others (such as your parents, friends or teammates). Write your thoughts down in a personal journal.

- Rewrite one or two key verses in your own words.

- Outline what each verse is saying.

- Give each verse a one-word title that summarizes what it says.

Share

Talk with God about what you've learned. Also, take time each day to share with another person what you learned during that day's study. Having a daily training time is the key to spiritual development. If you commit to working through these 31 devotionals over the next month, you will establish this as a habit—one that will be vital to your growth in Christ.

If you are committed to establishing this daily training time with God, fill out the line below.

I will commit to establishing a daily habit of spending time with God.

_____

Signed   Today's Date

Writers

We have invited athletes, coaches and team chaplains from all levels (in addition to FCA staff) to contribute their time, talent and experience in writing these devotions. These writers come from diverse backgrounds and include representatives from a variety of sports, including baseball, soccer, basketball, football, lacrosse, track and field, and others. You can check out our writers' mini-biographies in the Contributors section at the end of the book.

Format

Ready   A verse or passage of Scripture that focuses or directs your heart and mind. Turn to the Scripture reference in your Bible and read it within the overall context of the passage.

Set   A teaching point (a story, training point or thought taken from a sports perspective) that draws a lesson from the passage.

Go Questions that will help you examine your heart and challenge you to apply God's truth to your life—on and off the field.

Workout Additional Scripture references to help you dig deeper.

Overtime A closing prayer that will help you commit to the Lord what you have learned.

Journal At the end of each devotion is a place for you to record your responses to the "Go" questions and list other thoughts that you have on the topic.

TO RECEIVE THE DAILY EMAIL DEVOTIONAL
"FCA's Impact Play," go to www.FCA.org.

DAILY DEVOTIONS FOR
PEAK PERFORMANCE

1

Misplaced Treasures

Ready

But God said to him, "You fool! This very night
your life is demanded of you. And the things you
have prepared—whose will they be?" That's how it
is with the one who stores up treasure for himself
and is not rich toward God.

LUKE 12:20-21

Set

If you're running to win, but you have only earthly
goals in mind, your victory will be short-lived.
It will be a withering type of thing. You have to
have spiritual goals in mind. Things do get in
the way of being excellent—things like pride
and self-centeredness—but you have to try to
keep those types of thoughts out. You have to
do everything as unto the Lord, understanding
what's spiritual and what's long-lasting.

I'm reminded of the Scripture passage about
the guy who had the barns, was very blessed,
and said he was going to build bigger barns to
store all of his wares. God said to him, "You're
a fool, because all these things will be taken
from you this very night."

Where is your soul? That's the thing that's going to last. Our priorities are misguided if we

think only in terms of individual excellence. Everything has to balance out. Excellence without service, or excellence without teamwork, is excellence for only your purpose. God has bigger and better things in store for you. —*Tony Dungy*

Go

1. What are some of your athletic goals? How much importance do you place on winning?

2. How can you apply the parable found in Luke 12:13-21 to your athletic dreams?

3. What are some ways that you can keep from becoming too prideful and over-confident following your successes?

Workout
Matthew 7:24-27; Luke 12:13-21;
1 Corinthians 9:24

Overtime
Lord, help me root out prideful, self-centered goals in my life and replace them with God-centered hopes and dreams that will bring You glory through service to others and a spirit of excellence in everything I do. Amen.

Journal

Journal

2

Fire in My Belly

Ready

The words are fire in my belly, a burning in my bones.
I'm worn out trying to hold it in. I can't do it any longer!

JEREMIAH 20:9, *THE MESSAGE*

Set

"Do you have fire in your belly?" I've heard this question hundreds of times from coaches. It was never really a question I was supposed to answer; rather, it was a challenge to play harder and tougher. Basically, coaches wanted to know if I had the passion and determination to play with a competitive edge.

As an athlete, I never had the natural ability of others (speed, strength, size), but I did have the fire in my belly. For me, the fire was hustle, grit and tenacity to get the job done—whatever Coach asked of me! I was the player who always gave 100 percent, right up until the whistle blew. My goal was to leave it all on the field during practice and during games.

Sometimes I wonder if I have the fire in my belly when it comes to my spiritual life. Jeremiah says he had a fire burning so strongly for God that he couldn't contain it. The spiritual hustle, the spiritual grit, and the spiritual tenacity all need to burn within us so fiercely that we can't hold them back. Can you imagine finally confessing to a teammate, "I'm tired of withholding Jesus from you. It's burning so strongly inside of me that I have no choice but to share Jesus with you"? That would be incredible!

Our passion for the Lord should be like a fire that rages within us. However, we must also remember that the fire comes from Him. We must lay ourselves on the altar and ask God to consume us with His fire. The great preacher John Wesley said that large crowds came to hear him preach during the Great Awakening because "I set myself on fire and people come to watch me burn." Are you on fire for Jesus?
—*Dan Britton*

Go

1. What do you think of when you hear the phrase "a spiritual fire in the belly"?

2. What does it mean to have spiritual grit and tenacity?

3. What do you think would happen if you confessed to your teammates that you are tired of withholding Jesus from them?

Workout
Psalm 84:1-2

Overtime

*Lord, I have competitive fire in my belly,
but I also want that spiritual fire.
Consume me with Your fire, Jesus. Let the
fire that burns within me be a light in the
darkness that surrounds me. Amen.*

Journal

Journal

In the Light

Ready

God is light, and there is absolutely no darkness in Him. If we say, "We have fellowship with Him," and walk in darkness, we are lying and are not practicing the truth. But if we walk in the light as He Himself is in the light, we have fellowship with one another, and the blood of Jesus His Son cleanses us from all sin.

1 JOHN 1:5-7

Set

I don't know about you, but I don't want my life to be a lie. The Holy Spirit—through the apostle John—tells us that if we claim to be followers of Jesus Christ but live "in darkness," we are liars.

The other option is to "walk in the light," as Jesus did when He was on the earth. If we are faithful in doing so, two things are granted to us: fellowship with other believers and continual cleansing from sin. Sharing life with others who know Jesus is important; God did not create us to be alone! When we "walk in the light," the dark parts of our lives are revealed, giving us the opportunity to correct them, repent and move forward, and allowing us to grow closer to our Father along the way.

Let the light of Jesus shine on your life, and encourage fellow believers to do the same. When we do this, we can have a dynamic relationship with Jesus—and He impacts our lives more and more deeply as the Holy Spirit uses the Word of God to transform us. Imagine the world we would live in if we would let His light shine.
—*Daniel Sepulveda*

Go

1. When have you tried to hide a mistake from your coach, parents or friends? How easy or difficult was it to "live a lie"?

2. How have you tried to keep secrets about your past? What bad things can happen when you try to hide bad decisions?

3. How can living a lie bleed into your relationship with Jesus? What are the dangers of falling into that trap? What can you do to avoid the temptation of "living a lie"?

Workout
Psalm 69:5; Matthew 25:31-45; John 8:1-11

Overtime
Lord, forgive me for living a lie. Uncover my sins and cleanse my soul. Give me strength to move forward and grace to walk in Your light. Amen.

Journal

Journal

4

Pick It Up

Ready

Though a righteous man falls seven times, he will get up, but the wicked will stumble into ruin.

PROVERBS 24:16

Set

Starting when I was a little kid, I always wondered what it took to be an Olympian. *What type of characteristics do you have to have? What kind of person do you have to be?* Now that I am one, I'm very humbled—because it's not like I feel that I'm so great, or that I've done anything so special to deserve to get to the Olympics.

I feel like the thing I've done best is simply to get back up from all of the lickings I've taken, both physically and spiritually. I'm a pretty black-and-white person. I'll try to live the best I can; then I'll mess up and fall, and I'll get upset with myself. I've learned over the years not to let myself get as emotionally down when I mess up, and I try to pick myself up off the ground more quickly after making a mistake.

I love what the Bible states in Proverbs 24:16. This verse really inspires me, because I feel like it summarizes a lot of my physical and spiritual journeys to this point. I'm definitely not perfect by any stretch, but when I rely on God's strength, I know that I can pick myself up and keep moving forward. —*Ryan Hall*

Go

1. What do you think are some of the characteristics it takes to become an elite athlete?

2. Can you describe a time in your athletic career when you literally stumbled and fell? How did you react to that mishap?

3. As an athlete, what motivates you to keep moving forward after making a mistake? How does that determination translate to your everyday life and your Christian walk?

Workout
Philippians 3:12-14; Hebrews 10:35-38

Overtime
Lord, thank You for the grace that You extend when I stumble and fall. Help me to rely on Your perfect strength so that I might be able to pick myself up and press on toward the ultimate prize. Amen.

Journal

Journal

5

Sweat Equity

Ready

*You intended to harm me, but God intended it
for good to accomplish what is now being done,
the saving of many lives.*

GENESIS 50:20, *NIV*

Set

A mutual respect exists among athletes. To
some degree, as athletes we all have a single-
minded, committed lifestyle that is laced with
challenges. This is the price we pay to excel. An
athlete's identity and purpose hinge on his or
her performance, but what happens when adversity strikes?

What we see as adversity, God sees as opportunity. In Genesis 38–39, we read the story of
how Joseph was sold into slavery by his own
family and then imprisoned for 13 years for a
crime he did not commit. But Joseph stood
firm. "What men meant for evil, God used for
good," he said (see Genesis 50:20). Joseph was
right: Years after being sold into slavery, he be-
came second-in-command over all of Egypt!

Adversity not only builds character, but it
also reveals it. In 1 Samuel 17, David, who was
deemed too young to go to battle with his eight

older brothers, cultivated his skills by fighting lions and bears while tending his flock. Then, armed with only a sling and stones, this small shepherd boy faced the giant that no other Israelite soldier dared to fight.

"You come against me with a dagger, spear, and sword," David said to the giant, "but I come against you in the name of the Lord of Hosts, the God of Israel's armies—you have defied Him. Today, the Lord will hand you over to me" (1 Samuel 17:45-46). David declared that the battle was the Lord's, and he defeated the mighty Goliath.

Playing ball meant the world to me as a young man. God had blessed me with natural ability, and I excelled at every level. Then adversity struck. I was cut by the first NFL team that signed me. Down and out, I begrudgingly headed to Tampa Bay to play for the Bandits of the USFL. It was there that I met Jesus through the Bandits' chapel program. God then called me to youth ministry.

I am living proof that God can do great things with what we consider discouraging situations. Whether we have been deceived, beaten, jailed, surrounded by lions, or cut from a team, we are being prepared through adversities for divine opportunity! —*Harry Flaherty*

Go

1. What adversities and challenges are you currently facing in your life?

2. What is being revealed about your character in the midst of these adversities?

3. How will you choose to view the adversities you are facing?

Workout
Genesis 50:15-21; 1 Samuel 17:45-47; Psalm 23

Overtime
Father, help me today to draw upon Your strength when facing adversity. Use these situations for Your glory and Your purpose. Amen.

Journal

Journal

6

Modeling Christ

Ready

Be imitators of me, as I also am of Christ.
1 CORINTHIANS 11:1

Set

As Christians, we need to model Christ and show people what life is all about. Life is not just about taking, getting, receiving or taking advantage of opportunities that are presented to you; it is also about helping and serving others.

Jesus did some things in the course of His ministry to show the disciples why He was here—what His mission was—and He said, "Let this be an example to you." For instance, He washed their feet so they would understand that He came as a servant and that they were supposed to serve one another as well. Role modeling was an important part of His ministry.

Our job as Christians is to be a role model for those around us. That's where you should find satisfaction—from knowing that you have helped someone. —*Tony Dungy*

Go

1. Name some athletes after whom you try to model yourself. What particular

characteristics of theirs are most appealing to you and why?

2. What are some of the characteristics Jesus displayed while He lived on earth? What challenges do you face in trying to model your life after those characteristics?

3. Why do you think Paul challenged the believers to imitate him as he imitated Christ? What might be some of the benefits of modeling Christ for others?

Workout
John 13:1-17; 1 Peter 2:19-25

Overtime
Lord, help me know the character of Jesus. Let Your Holy Spirit give me strength and understanding so that I might model that character for those around me. Amen.

Journal

Journal

7

Endurance

Ready

Rejoice in hope; be patient in affliction;
be persistent in prayer.
ROMANS 12:12

Set

Endurance means putting one foot in front of the other, no matter how things are going. At the London Marathon, some of the hardest parts of the race were talking myself through the rough patches. The marathon is a good analogy for life in general. You're going to go through those difficult stretches where you don't feel good. You can either get down on yourself and cave in and start doing poorly, or you can tell yourself that you're going to do your best no matter how you're feeling or how slowly you started. I really had to mentally coach myself through some rough patches in that race, and I think that's a core element of endurance.

Tough times are inevitable. They're going to come. But you have to keep pushing on, because you know you have a big hope.

The Bible states that Christ endured the cross for the joy set before Him (see Hebrews 12:2). There's a prize waiting for each of us at

the end of the race. If we fix our eyes on that prize, we will be able to endure things we never thought we could possibly go through.
—*Ryan Hall*

Go

1. As an athlete, can you think of any instances when you had to endure tough times or perhaps painful situations en route to achieving your goals? From where did you find the strength to push through those challenges?

2. According to Romans 12:12, what characteristics are vital when it comes to endurance? Why does that advice seem to go against human nature?

3. What gives you hope? What biblical promises make it easier for you to endure troublesome times in your life?

Workout
John 17:1-4; 2 Timothy 2:11-13

Overtime
Lord, give me the joy, patience and persistent desire to pray no matter what difficult situations I face. Grant me the strength and endurance to push through to the end of the race. Amen.

Journal

Journal

8

One Way 2 Play

Ready

*Be strong and very courageous. Be careful to obey
all the law my servant Moses gave you; do not turn
from it to the right or to the left, that you may be
successful wherever you go.*
JOSHUA 1:7, *NIV*

Set

Most students who find themselves in situations or places they hoped they'd never be do so because of tiny compromises that they made early in their life journeys. I have never met a student who identified alcoholism as a career goal. Neither have I met an ambitious student whose "Top 10 Things to Do Before Graduation" included becoming a parent prematurely, getting kicked off a team, or losing the trust and respect of their parents.

Although most students want to avoid these misfortunes like the plague, many engage in behaviors that increase the probability that they will experience these situations. These compromises are common among all teens—black or white, rich or poor, and regardless of whether they live in the city or the suburbs.

Almost always, the common denominator is drug use. It doesn't matter if it's a cigarette here or there; an occasional beer or hard liquor drink; or weed, blunts, ecstasy or heroin. Drugs will always diminish the masterpiece that is you! You are a miracle of God. When you are high or enhanced, the end result of what you've smoked, drunk, popped or huffed will always be defeat.

Most of those who compromise do so because of the absence of three things: *faith, commitment* and *accountability*. I am so glad that when I was a teen, I had *faith* enough to believe that if I did what was right, all the right things in life would come back to me. I am glad that I had the courage and strength to *commit* to being drug-free and not turn to the left or right of that commitment. I'm also glad that I surrounded myself with like-minded people who held me *accountable* to my commitments.
—*Steve Fitzhugh*

Go

1. What is your view on alcohol and drug use? Do you agree that using drugs will diminish the masterpiece that is you?

2. Are you compromising in the area of drug and alcohol use? If so, how?

3. What decisions will you make with regard to faith, commitment and ac-

countability to follow God's "one way 2 play"—drug and alcohol free?

Workout

Joshua 1:9; Psalm 84:11; 1 Corinthians 6:19-20; Hebrews 12:1-2

Overtime

God, give me strength as I make this commitment to remain drug free. Help me identify an accountability partner— someone who will encourage me to be faithful to my commitment and who will ask me the tough questions I need to hear. Amen.

Journal

Journal

9

The Competitor's Prayer

Ready

Pour out your hearts before Him. God is our refuge.
PSALM 62:8

Set

Many times, pre-game prayers can be a "rah-rah" talk or a desperate plea to God for a big win. But as true competitors, we need to ask ourselves, *What is the proper way to pray before entering the battle? How should we pour out our hearts before God so that we will be spiritually ready for competition?* Here is a great prayer that you can pray before a game, competition, workout or practice:

"Lord, I compete for You alone. In every victory and every loss, I play for You. Every time I compete, I stand for the cross. My love for the game is evidence of my love for You. I play for You, Lord. When I put on the uniform, lace up the shoes, and walk out of the locker room, I declare my loyalty to You.

"My drive comes from the Holy Spirit. Through the pain and through the cheers, I will not give in or give up. My passion for competition comes from above. I sweat for the One who made me. The champion inside of me is Jesus. My only goal is to glorify the name of Christ. To win is to honor Him.

"I feel Your delight when I compete. All of my abilities are from You, Jesus. My heart yearns for Your applause. I am under Your authority. I will respect and honor my teammates, coaches and opponents. I will play by the rules. I will submit to You as my ultimate Coach.

"I am Your warrior in the heat of battle. I am humble in victory and gracious in defeat. I serve those on my team and those I compete against. My words inspire and motivate. I utter what You desire. My body is Your temple; nothing enters my body that is not honoring to You. I train to bring You glory. My sweat is an offering to my heavenly Master.

"I wear Your jersey, Lord. Victory does not lie in winning, but in becoming more like You. There is no greater victory. In Your name, I pray. Amen." —*Dan Britton*

Go

1. What are your pre-game prayers like?

2. Do you define winning by the scoreboard or by Christlike competition?

3. How can you develop your prayer life in the arena of competition?

Workout
Mark 11:24-25; Matthew 6:5-7

Overtime
*Lord, I admit that my prayers before
competition are often more focused on the
scoreboard than on becoming like You.
I desire to pour out my heart before
You every day that I compete. Develop in
me a pure heart. Amen.*

Journal

Journal

10

Defeating Jealousy

Ready

*So rid yourselves of all wickedness, all deceit,
hypocrisy, envy, and all slander.*

1 PETER 2:1

Set

Jealousy can destroy a team. Often it starts with outside people saying, "You could do this and you should do that," or "The only reason you can't do it is because that other player is getting two more shots than you are."

It's funny when you think about it, but if you're not careful, you'll start buying into it and saying to yourself, *Yeah, I should be playing more.* But whatever God has for you, you will have. Nobody else can take that away. If you're not getting the playing time or the recognition you should get, work harder. Don't sit there and blame somebody else for what they're doing.

You always hear about people who say, "I'm waiting for God to do something in my life," while they're sitting on the couch at home. It's hard for God to make a move if you're not putting out the effort. As Proverbs 14:23 states, "There is profit in all hard work, but endless talk leads only to poverty." —*Tamika Catchings*

Go

1. Can you describe a time when jealousy undermined a team on which you were playing?

2. What are some sources of jealousy with which you have struggled? How did that jealousy impact your performance and the overall success of the team?

3. How does Proverbs 14:23 speak to those who are tempted to compare themselves to others? Read 1 Corinthians 13:4-5. What does this Scripture passage suggest is the ultimate remedy for jealousy?

Workout
James 3:13-18; 1 Peter 2:1-3

Overtime
Lord, help me ward off jealousy with a strong work ethic and God-centered love and respect for my teammates. Amen.

Journal

Journal

11

Strength in Numbers

Ready

A wise warrior is better than a strong one,
and a man of knowledge than one of strength;
for you should wage war with sound guidance—
victory comes with many counselors.

PROVERBS 24:5-6

Set

There are several people who mentor me and speak into my life. If I have an issue, I have five mentors on whom I can call, and they all give me different perspectives. It takes many advisers to win the war. That doesn't mean we should ask 100 people for advice. But it's important to have godly counsel poured into your life; your friends' wisdom will help keep your steps straight.

When it comes to accountability, I definitely believe in strength in numbers. If some issues are popping up, we can all come together in agreement and pull one another out of a bad situation. That's a powerful thing.

A lot of times, we don't surround ourselves with enough people. We might just have one friend whom we consult. When a problem arises (drinking, for example), the one struggling might ask the other to help—and the next thing you know, the first one has pulled his friend down with him. But if there are three brothers around, they're going to work together to pull the struggling person up. —*Shaun Alexander*

Go

1. How does the phrase "strength in numbers" relate to your sport?

2. Can you describe a time when you tried to do things on your own? Can you describe a time when you relied on the advice and counsel of others? What were the outcomes of the two situations?

3. As a Christian, what are some scenarios in which having "strength in numbers" might make the difference between success and failure?

Workout

Proverbs 12:1; Matthew 18:19-20; James 5:16

Overtime

Lord, help me to resist the temptation of going it alone. Surround me with wise believers of integrity who can counsel and guide me in Your ways. Amen.

Journal

Journal

12

$10 Million Tongue

Ready

*With the tongue we praise our Lord and Father,
and with it we curse men, who have been made in
God's likeness. Out of the same mouth come praise
and cursing. My brothers, this should not be.*
JAMES 3:9-10, *NIV*

Set

As competitors, it is often hard for us to guard our mouths. Carson Palmer, a Heisman Trophy winner and the number one NFL draft pick in 2003, signed a $49 million, 6-year contract with the Cincinnati Bengals.

A total of $10 million of the deal was for his signing bonus.

However, that $10 million wasn't contingent upon his strong throwing arm, his intelligence as a quarterback, or his great play calling. It was contingent upon his tongue and whether or not he would say anything negative about his team, coaches or management. Basically, the $10 million signing bonus was a loyalty pledge in which Carson guaranteed that he would not be critical. If he ripped into his team, he lost the cash. This was quite an incentive for him to keep his speech positive and encouraging.

In the heat of battle, it is difficult to keep our tongues from slipping. After someone has wronged us on the field or in the locker room, it is easy to lash out. God desires that we not only keep our mouths from cursing but also abstain from being critical.

There are two types of people in the world: builders and tearers. Builders use their words to lift up those around them. They make other people feel good about themselves. They pour into the emotional bank accounts of others. Tearers are people who berate those around them. They are the cut-down kings, usually saying things to make themselves look better in front of others.

The bottom line is that the tongue is only a reflection of what is in the heart. When the pressure comes, we speak what is in our hearts. When you are under pressure, what comes out? Criticism or godliness? You might not get paid $10 million for having a Christlike tongue, but your Savior will be glorified! *—Dan Britton*

Go

1. What kind of person are you—a builder or a tearer? Which one would your friends and teammates say you are?

2. What came out of your heart the last time you were under pressure? How will you respond similarly or differently next time?

3. What does it mean to have a Christlike tongue? What are some specific ways that you could change what comes out of your mouth?

Workout

Proverbs 12:18; Proverbs 15:4; Ephesians 4:29;
1 Peter 3:10

Overtime

*Lord, help me to be a person whose words
build up those around me—those in my family,
in my school, on my team and in my neighborhood.
Create in me a clean heart, God. I desire to
glorify You in all I say. Amen.*

Journal

Journal

13

Vow of Integrity

Ready

I will pay attention to the way of integrity.
When will You come to me? I will live with
integrity of heart in my house.

PSALM 101:2

Set

Integrity isn't just something you display when you're out in public or on the job. It also carries over to your family, to your kids, to your neighbors—to everybody who comes into contact with you.

Do I tell my family, "This is what I want you to do," but I don't do the things I ask of them? Do I say, "This is what we're going to be all about as a family," but then next week I change my mind? Such inconsistencies are very confusing. It's important to let my family know that we have certain standards—the Lord's standards. Those are what we're going to try to live up to.

Sure, we're going to fail at times, and we're going to fall short, but this is what we need to be about. If you're not totally transparent and honest with those closest to you—if you don't have that integrity at home—then it's going to cause problems there sooner than it does in public. —*Tony Dungy*

Go

1. What are some examples of how one's level of integrity might change depending on the surroundings or the circumstances?

2. What are some dangers that might come from having inconsistent character?

3. What are some ways that you can avoid the temptation of living one way in public and another way in private? What are the benefits of committing to a lifestyle of integrity?

Workout
Psalms 101; 139:23-24

Overtime
Lord, I want to live a life of integrity in private and in public. Help me to be the same person of moral, biblical character no matter where I go, no matter who is around, and no matter what challenging circumstances I might face along the way. Amen.

Journal

Journal

Far More Important

Ready

*Love the Lord your God with all your heart,
with all your soul, with all your mind, and with all
your strength. . . . Love your neighbor as yourself.
There is no other commandment greater than these.*

MARK 12:30-31

Set

As a young athlete, I thought winning was every-thing. I wanted to win every time I competed. Whether it was a big high school game against our rivals or just a pick-up basketball game against my brothers, I wanted to win. The com-petitive juices would always flow through me. One of the greatest NFL coaches of all time, Vin-cent Lombardi, once said, "Winning isn't every-thing—but wanting to win is." As an athlete, I had a lot of wanting, even though I didn't win every time.

In Mark 12:33, a religious teacher summa-rized Jesus' words by saying, "To love Him with all your heart, with all your understanding, and with all your strength, and to love your neigh-bor as yourself, is far more important than all the burnt offerings and sacrifices." At that time, burnt offerings and sacrifices were important.

But this man realized that there was nothing more important than loving God.

What could possibly be more important to us than loving God? Maybe for you it's not burnt offerings, but it could be your sport, your friends, your family, schoolwork, the future, or maybe even winning. Usually, there is something in our lives that tries to crowd out Jesus. Examine your heart today and ask God to show you what is keeping you from loving Him above all else. —*Dan Britton*

Go

1. Is there anything or anyone in your life more important than Jesus?

2. Would your best friend agree with your answer to the above question? What do you think Jesus would say?

3. Vince Lombardi shared his perspective on winning. What would be your personal definition of winning?

Workout
Deuteronomy 6:4-9

Overtime
Lord, I want nothing in my life to be more important than You. So many things try to crowd You out. Pour out Your wisdom and help me to see what those things are. You are first in my life. You are far more important than anything. Amen.

Journal

Journal

15

What God Hates

Ready

Six things the Lord hates; in fact, seven are detestable to Him: arrogant eyes, a lying tongue, hands that shed innocent blood, a heart that plots wicked schemes, feet eager to run to evil, a lying witness who gives false testimony, and one who stirs up trouble among brothers.

PROVERBS 6:16-19

Set

What enters your mind as you read the verses above, knowing that God hates the behaviors listed there? Do you find yourself thinking of times, perhaps even recently, when you have done something that God abhors? It's interesting (and convicting) that the Lord puts shedding innocent blood and spreading strife among brothers on the same list. To the world, shedding innocent blood is certainly considered much worse than creating conflict. But just what does it mean to stir up "trouble among brothers"?

"Strife" is defined as "a bitter, sometimes violent conflict or dissension; an act of contention; exertion or contention for superiority." On a sports team, this could take many forms. It could be a situation in which you turn one of your teammates against another player so that you'll end up on top. Even if the argument or hard feelings only exist between you and one other person, everyone on your team feels the tension, and that leads to strife.

Consider how you're treating your teammates and the other people in your life. If you're creating strife, ask the Lord for wisdom. Ask Him to show you how to behave differently, and then act on the guidance He gives you. Also, talk to an adult whom you respect and who treats people with the respect and kindness you want to exhibit. —*Roxanne Robbins*

Go

1. Are you involved in any kind of strife on your team?

2. Are you the one creating this strife?

3. How can you mend the situation based on the principles that God teaches us in the Bible?

Workout
Matthew 5:21-24; 1 Thessalonians 4:1-12

Overtime
Father, as I read Proverbs 6:16-19, I am reminded that many of my actions are abhorred by You. I am guilty of manipulating my teammates and friends to get what I want. Please forgive me and show me the way to correct these actions. Cause them to be as detestable to me as they are to You. I pray all this in Your name. Amen.

Journal

Journal

16

In His Eyes

Ready

*My soul, praise the Lord, and all that is within me,
praise His holy name. My soul, praise the Lord, and do
not forget all His benefits. He forgives all your sin;
He heals all your diseases. He redeems your life
from the Pit; He crowns you with faithful love and
compassion. He satisfies you with goodness;
your youth is renewed like the eagle.*

PSALM 103:1-5

Set

If you tried to count on your hands the number of times someone has let you down or you have let someone else down, you'd run out of fingers. As humans, we fail miserably all the time. Thankfully, there are promises in the Bible such as the one in Psalm 103:12: "As far as the east is from the west, so far has He removed our transgressions from us."

There is incredible power in looking at ourselves through the eyes of Christ. No matter the mistake, the loss, the pain or the regret, in God's eyes we shine brightly. When you feel inadequate, depressed or ashamed, feel His presence. He redeems your life, rescues you from the pit, and showers you with love and compassion.

He satisfies your desires with awesome and wonderful things.

No matter where you've been or what you've done, God can restore you. Take a peek at yourself through His eyes—the eyes of grace and love.
—*Danny Burns*

Go

1. What causes you to be ashamed of actions you have taken in your life?

2. Do you realize that you are loved by God, and that He has forgiven you?

3. What can you do to become the bright creation that God sees?

Workout
Luke 15:1-7; Romans 5:1-11

Overtime
God, it's so hard to fathom the pain in Your eyes as You watch me do what You despise. Yet through it all, Lord, Your love endures forever. Your grace and mercy are unexplainable. Lord, change me. Draw me close to You, Jesus, and restore me. Amen.

Who is a God like You, removing iniquity and passing over rebellion for the remnant of His inheritance?

He does not hold on to His anger forever,
because He delights in faithful love.

He will again have compassion on us;
He will vanquish our iniquities.
You will cast all our sins
into the depths of the sea
(Micah 7:18-19).

Journal

Journal

17

No Comparison

Ready
Let us fix our eyes on Jesus.
HEBREWS 12:2, *NIV*

Set
I had set my blocks for the 110-meter hurdles and taken a couple of practice starts. The starter called out, "Runners to your marks!" In my pre-race nervousness, I turned to my left and right to compare myself to the other runners. It was then that I noticed that the line I was using for the start was a full meter behind all of the other runners. I made the fateful decision to keep my feet in my blocks while moving both hands up even with the other runners. I was nearly lying flat when the gun went off. I crawled out of the blocks and hit almost every hurdle. I finished second to last!

Where did I go wrong? I took my eyes off the finish line and began to compare myself with the other runners. I was trying to compete the way that others were competing instead of running my own race.

In sports, it is easy to compare ourselves to others rather than play our individual games in the way that we have practiced. We try to make someone else's unique ways our ways. But focusing on another person's game prevents us from focusing on our own games and competing the way that God created us to compete. This does not mean that we should have the mentality of a loner and neglect the team for our personal benefit; rather, competing the way that God created us to compete means that we work to develop our unique skills so that we can be the best that we have been created to be.

Spiritually speaking, when do we get off track? When we take our eyes off Jesus—the finish line—and begin comparing ourselves to others. Stop the comparisons and play your game. Compete the way you have prepared to compete. Be committed to developing your skills and your unique abilities so that your game is at its best and you reach the finish line having run *your* race. —*Kerry O'Neill*

Go

1. In what areas are you comparing yourself to others rather than fixing your eyes on Christ?

2. Why do you think you are making this comparison?

3. How does this negatively affect your spiritual life?

Workout
Psalm 18:29-30; Mark 8:34-35;
Colossians 3:23-24

Overtime
*Lord, thank You for making me
a unique creation. Help me to delight
in that uniqueness today and to use
the abilities You have given me in the
way that You see fit. Amen.*

Journal

Journal

18

Driven

Ready

Therefore, be imitators of God, as dearly loved children.
EPHESIANS 5:1

Set

When it comes to excellence, I try to look at everything through God's eyes. I look to Jesus as the ultimate example of excellence, service and humility—as well as many other values. Though I strive to imitate Him, obviously I fall short in every category in comparison to Him. His example is the pure definition of excellence.

Our excellence begins with looking at Jesus and His life. When you look at the Christian faith and who we are as people, it's clear that we all fall short of Christ's example. But that doesn't mean we should stop striving for excellence. If we give up on that, we miss an important concept that Jesus teaches us.

Especially in sports, there is often a misconception that Christian athletes are too nice or don't want to compete. But for me, competition is part of my faith. It's about competing as hard as I can for God's glory. It's not for my glory but for where He wants to take me in life. That's really what drives me to continue. —*Chris Klein*

Go

1. What is your definition of excellence? What drives you to be competitive and excellent?

2. What are some specific areas that require excellence in order to succeed as an athlete? What daily steps have you taken to achieve those goals?

3. How often do you measure your pursuit of excellence against the life of Christ? What aspects of Christ's character inspire you to give your best?

Workout
Romans 3:21-28; 1 Peter 2:19-25

Overtime
Lord, teach me the true meaning of excellence as displayed through the life of Jesus Christ. Give me the strength and drive to emulate His example in everything I do.
Amen.

Journal

Journal

19

Team Player

Ready

Then he called the crowd to him along with his disciples and said: "If anyone would come after me, he must deny himself and take up his cross and follow me. For whoever wants to save his life will lose it, but whoever loses his life for me and for the gospel will save it.

MARK 8:34-35, *NIV*

Set

We were having an inter-squad scrimmage, and I was standing among a group of athletes, waiting to find out which team I would be on. I was sure that I would be placed on the team with the best athletes in the school—who were also my best friends.

Instead, I was chosen to join a team that was considered to be the underdogs. In my anger and disgust, I told the coach that I was going to quit and began walking off of the field.

To my surprise, the coach let me go. I had been so sure that he would try to stop me, but he didn't. As I continued walking away slowly, I started thinking, *What am I going to tell my parents? And what are my friends going to think of me?*

Suddenly, I came to my senses, went back and joined the team. Guess what? Our team won the scrimmage, and I apologized to the coach for not trusting that he knew what he was doing.

We must always remember to look at the big picture. It's not about us, and it's not about what we want. Being on God's team means denying what we want and following Him. He strategically places us in the situations in life in which we can make the greatest impact. Sometimes this means being separated from things that we want and the people who are most familiar to us.

Remember, you have been created to make a difference, and your team's ability to win may just lie within you. —*Carl Miller*

Go

1. What traits do you bring to your team that will make a difference?

2. Can you think of a situation that you thought would be the worst experience of your life but turned out to be one of the best?

3. How willing are you to give up your rights and desires for the sake of your team?

Workout
Mark 10:29-30; John 15:16;
1 Corinthians 1:27-29

Overtime

God, help me to deny my own selfish desires, even when I am placed in situations that are not comfortable for me. I want to bring You honor in all that I do. Help me to look past what I want so that I can use the talent that You have given me to make a difference for the team on which I have been placed. Amen.

Journal

Journal

20

True Identity

Ready

For in Him the entire fullness of God's nature dwells bodily, and you have been filled by Him, who is the head over every ruler and authority.

COLOSSIANS 2:9-10

Set

The world's definition of *excellence* is based strictly on performance. As soon as you're not performing, no one in the media wants to talk to you anymore, and it's easy to get down on yourself. Identity gets all wrapped up in performance.

It's like building your house on the sand. That kind of foundation is very changing and fleeting—eventually it's going to be gone, because no one is always on top of his or her game. But when you find your identity in Christ and in what He's done for you, your foundation is on the unchanging, sturdy rock that you can always stand on. You can have a much healthier perspective on yourself and life in general—and on the source of your hope. When I'm not performing well, I lose my hope. I lose my joy. I get down. I get depressed. But when you find your identity in Christ, that's unchanging. No matter what you do, you can't mess that up.

Excellence is getting back up after you've fallen. It's knowing that your true value is in Christ and that He is our hope for the future. He is our everything—and who we are is based on that, not on our performance. —*Ryan Hall*

Go

1. How much does your athletic performance affect your emotions and your attitude? Why do you think that is so?

2. As an athlete, by what words do you like to be identified? Why are those descriptions important to you?

3. What does the phrase "find your identity in Christ" mean to you? How might accepting the premise of Colossians 2:9-10—that "the entire fullness of God's nature dwells bodily" within those who believe in Jesus—change the way you approach performance?

Workout
John 14:12; 15:15; Romans 8:15-17

Overtime
Lord, help me understand what it means to find my identity in Christ. Help me not to be so wrapped up in my performance, but instead to have a balanced approach to athletics and everything I do in life.
Amen.

Journal

Journal

21

Personal Best

Ready

*God has put the body together, giving greater honor to
the less honorable, so that there would be no division in
the body, but that the members would have the same
concern for each other. So if one member suffers, all the
members suffer with it; if one member is honored, all
the members rejoice with it. Now you are the body of
Christ, and individual members of it.*

1 CORINTHIANS 12:24-27

Set

What position is the most important in the
game of football? What about in volleyball? In
baseball? There is a common misconception in
team sports that the most important position
on a team is the one played by the person who
gets the most headlines or touches the ball the
most. However, these are not always the most
important roles on a team.

So what is the most important role? The answer is simple: It's the one that you have been
asked to play. God's Word states that whatever
you are asked to do, you should do it with all
your might (see Ecclesiastes 9:10).

If you are playing offensive guard, and you
don't block your assignment, the whole team
pays the price. If you are a second stringer, and

you don't put forth your best effort in practice, the whole team suffers. In volleyball, the hitters will never even touch the ball without a good pass from the back row.

Paul tells us in 1 Corinthians 12 that a body cannot function as it was designed to function unless its many parts work together. We should not consider one part of the body to be more important than another, nor should we believe that whatever role we have been asked to play is insignificant.

In both sports and life, the most important role is the one that you are asked to play. It is significant. Give your best on each and every play. The team is depending on you! —*Joe Outlaw*

Go

1. What is your role on your team or in your line of work? What are your primary roles in life?

2. Have you ever felt that your role was not important? Have you considered whether your role would even exist if it weren't important?

3. According to Scripture, how should your attitude regarding your role in life change?

Workout
1 Corinthians 12:12-27; Colossians 3:17,23-24

Overtime

*Lord, thank You that I am on Team Jesus
Christ. You have blessed me with gifts
and talents, and I want to use them on
Your team. I am grateful that I am one of
a kind, and that nobody else can play the
role I can. Thank You, Jesus, for blessing
me and giving me the privilege to serve.
Amen.*

Journal

Journal

22

Whose Side?

Ready

When Joshua was near Jericho, he looked up and saw a
man standing in front of him with a drawn sword in
His hand. Joshua approached Him and asked, "Are You
for us or for our enemies?" "Neither," He replied.
"I have now come as commander of the Lord's army."

JOSHUA 5:13-14

Set

After playing in and coaching thousands of
games, I have found that I struggle with one
main issue: Whose team is God on—my team or
the other team? How can God pick sides? If He
does pick sides, how does He decide which side
to be on? If there are Christians on both teams,
then how can God be on both teams? These
questions challenge us as athletes and coaches.

Let me be honest with you. When I compete,
I want God to be solely on my team and not on
the other team! However, when we have that
mind-set, we have it all wrong. In the Bible,
Joshua, the commander of Israel's army, was
preparing his troops for battle against Jericho
when the commander of the Lord's army appeared to him. When Joshua asked him whose
side he was on, the commander of the Lord's
army replied, "Neither."

Does this mean that God doesn't take sides? Well, there is a bigger issue here. It's not whether the Lord is on our team or their team; it's whether or not we are on God's team! When we compete, we need to recognize that we are on Team Jesus Christ. It is human nature to want God to stand on our sideline. However, God wants us to be on His side only! —*Dan Britton*

Go

1. How can you apply the concept of being on God's team (rather than God being on your team) the next time you compete or practice?

2. What impact could it make on your team if all of your teammates understood this concept?

3. Why is it so difficult for us to remember that God's team is the only team that matters?

Workout
Ephesians 5:1-10

Overtime
Lord, help me to remember that I am on Your team and that it's not about You being on my team. Give me the proper mind-set to play for You. Every time I step onto the field of competition, I will wear Your uniform. Amen.

Journal

Journal

23

Athletes and Purity

Ready

*Do you not know that your body is a temple
of the Holy Spirit, who is in you, whom you
have received from God?*

1 CORINTHIANS 6:19, *NIV*

Set

An important question for any athlete to consider is, "What does God think about my sex life?" After all, it is to the heavenly Umpire that we must one day give an account!

God is not a cosmic killjoy. He wants us to enjoy life. He wants us to have a great sex life! But the Creator knows and has told us the time and place for everything. Sexual relations with a permanent spouse is God's plan. The apostle Paul tells us, "It is God's will that you should be sanctified [set apart to Him]: that you should avoid sexual immorality; that each of you should learn to control his own body in a way that is holy and honorable" (1 Thessalonians 4:3-4, *NIV*).

As athletes, most of us consider ourselves to be independent, self-sufficient and able to handle anything. But 1 Corinthians 10:12 says, "So, if you think you are standing firm, be careful that you don't fall!" (*NIV*). We are really not as strong as we think!

Frankly, the majority of movies, television shows and secular videos are trash. The world's music is full of suggestive lyrics that influence listeners. Spiritually, the mind that dwells on impure thoughts soon begins to rationalize, compromise and finally lose control. As Christian athletes, we must control our minds and replace any impure thoughts with thoughts of things that are pure. —*Elliot Johnson*

Go

1. As an athlete, what sexual pressures do you face? How are you tempted by what you see, hear, talk about or do?

2. How might giving in to sexual pressure distract you from your game?

3. What will you choose to do when tempted?

Workout

1 Corinthians 6:18; 2 Timothy 2:22;
1 Peter 2:11; 1 John 1:9

Overtime

Father, I am bombarded each day by outside influences that encourage me to do things that do not honor You. I realize that sexual purity requires more than just abstaining from sex—it requires that

I guard my mind as well as my actions. Grow in me the discernment and strength I need to turn away from things that cause me to stray from a standard of purity that brings You honor. Amen.

Journal

Journal

24

Protect the House

Ready

Therefore, brothers, by the mercies of God, I urge you to present your bodies as a living sacrifice, holy and pleasing to God; this is your spiritual worship.

ROMANS 12:1

Set

When the NFL's Baltimore Ravens are getting ready to go into battle, the stadium sound system blasts music, and the giant screens exhort the team to "Protect this House." This same scene is replayed week after week in stadiums all around the league. In the history of sports, there has never been a team that has liked losing on their home field. That is why most homecoming games are scheduled against competition that the home team should easily defeat.

God refers to our bodies as His house. Because we are believers, the Holy Spirit actually lives inside of us. And God expects us to protect His house! This is a high standard, especially since we live in a culture that promotes winning above all else.

Because the pressure to win is so great, many athletes have resorted to trying just about anything that will take their game to the next level.

Each year, hundreds of athletes test positive for illegal or banned substances. Performance-enhancing drug use has become so prevalent that each major sport has established elaborate drug-testing policies with increasing penalties for offenders.

God calls us to a different standard. He does not want us to do anything that would cause harm to our bodies or bring dishonor to His name. The reputation of athletes who test positive for drug use is forever tarnished. For believers, the name and reputation of Jesus also will be harmed. When we resort to banned or illegal substances to improve our performance, we are basically putting our trust and confidence in those substances. We are saying that the power of God is not able to give us the discipline, the determination, the drive or the talent to compete at our best. —*Jimmy Page*

Go

1. What substances do you put in your body that might bring dishonor to the name of Christ?

2. What would Jesus think about what you are willing to do in order to succeed in your sport?

3. Are you willing to stop using any questionable substances or supplements today?

Workout
Romans 8:9-11; Philippians 1:20-21;
2 Timothy 1:7

Overtime
Lord, help me to realize that Your Holy Spirit
lives in me. Help me to protect Your house from
anything that is harmful to my body or that
dishonors Your name. Amen.

Journal

Journal

25

The Playbook

Ready

I have kept my feet from every evil path to follow Your word. I have not turned from Your judgments, for You Yourself have instructed me. How sweet Your word is to my taste—[sweeter] than honey to my mouth. I gain understanding from Your precepts; therefore I hate every false way. Your word is a lamp for my feet and a light on my path.

PSALM 119:101-105

Set

One of the common elements in all levels of football, from pee-wee to pro, is the playbook. The playbook contains the game plan that each team uses to try to overcome its opponent. Without it, teams and players would be in a state of confusion, not knowing what to do or where to go. On the other hand, no matter how good the playbook is, it's absolutely useless if the players don't study it and apply it on the field.

When it comes to life, there is no better playbook than the Word of God. The Bible contains everything we need to defeat the opposition (the devil). Although we may recognize that God has a plan for our lives, we often do not acknowledge that the devil also has a game plan for our lives—and his plan is in complete opposition to God's.

The devil's plan is to steal and kill and destroy our lives, while God's plan is to give us full and abundant life. "A thief comes only to steal and to kill and to destroy. I have come that they may have life and have it in abundance" (John 10:10).

In order for us to consistently overcome our life's adversary, we must (1) know what God's "playbook" says by reading and studying it, and (2) apply what it says to our lives. If we don't, we are playing right into the hands of our enemy.

I encourage you to study and apply God's "playbook"—the Bible—to your life this week so that you can avoid being sacked by the devil!
—*Josh Carter*

Go

1. How has following your team's playbook or game plan impacted your performance in competition?

2. How often do you turn to God's playbook—the Bible—for guidance?

3. What are some specific ways in which you can apply God's Word to your life today?

Workout
Matthew 7:24-27; Luke 11:28;
James 1:19-25

Overtime

*God, thank You for providing us with
a playbook for life—the Holy Bible.
I pray that as I spend time reading Your
Word, the promises and instructions in
this playbook will be written on my heart.
Help me to apply what I read in my
day-to-day life. Amen.*

Journal

Journal

26

Obstacles and Opportunities

Ready

"Send some men to explore the land of Canaan, which
I am giving to the Israelites. From each ancestral tribe
send one of its leaders." So at the LORD's command
Moses sent them out from the Desert of Paran.

NUMBERS 13:2-3, *NIV*

Set

When you walk onto a court to play a game, do
you immediately think that you're going to lose
or that you're going to win? Do you stare at
your opponents while they warm up and begin
to wonder why you even laced up your Nikes,
or do you focus on giving your all? Do you see
obstacles, or do you see opportunities?

In Numbers 13, a dozen spies were sent into
Canaan to check out the land. God had already
given the Israelites great victories in battle and
rescued them from tough situations. During
the 40 days that the spies were evaluating the
land, they could have seen a great opportunity,
but most of them didn't.

Only two guys, Joshua and Caleb, thought
the tribes of Israel could succeed in acquiring

the land. The rest of the team did what I think many of us would have done: "But the men who had gone up with him said, 'We can't attack those people; they are stronger than we are.' And they spread among the Israelites a bad report about the land they had explored" (Numbers 13:31-32, *NIV*). In other words, they saw an obstacle and a formidable opponent, and they said, "We don't think that we can do this!"

Well, that much is true. We can't, but God can. It's strange that the Israelites didn't remember the situations from which God had already delivered them and the victories He had granted. They also forgot that God had commanded them to go into the land and that He had promised to give it to them. These were His words: "Send some men to explore the land of Canaan, which I am giving to the Israelites" (Numbers 13:2, *NIV*).

God has already given us much. We only need to receive what He has promised. So often, we are like these Israelites when faced with challenging situations. But I pray that we can be more like Joshua and Caleb, who received and believed in the opportunity that God had given them. —*Fleceia Comeaux*

Go

1. What types of obstacles do you encounter when you are competing?

2. With God's help, how might these obstacles be turned into opportunities?

3. What practical steps can you take to increase your faith in God's plan for your life?

Workout
Numbers 13:26-30; Deuteronomy 31:8; 2 Corinthians 12:9

Overtime
Lord, help me to remember that through my doubt, I can see only obstacles, but through my faith in You, I can see opportunities. Allow me to increase this faith every day. Amen.

Journal

Journal

27

Surprising Strength

Ready

*I have great confidence in you; I have great pride
in you. I am filled with encouragement; I am overcome
with joy in all our afflictions.*

2 CORINTHIANS 7:4

Set

Have you ever been nervous before a big game?
Have you ever felt like quitting an event before
you even got started? The first time I competed
in the Boston Marathon, I didn't think I should
even be in the race. As I waited at the starting
line, in my mind I was yelling at my coach, *I
don't belong in this race! I'm not strong enough!*

However, one of the most amazing things
happened to me that day. Although on the
starting line I doubted my ability to even finish the famous Boston Marathon, 26 miles later
I had won the race and broken the world record
by almost 7 minutes! I was stronger than I
thought I was!

When the Israelites were preparing to enter
the land of Canaan, they were most likely also
a bit nervous. Moses had died, and they were
now under the leadership of Joshua. However,

God told them to be strong and courageous, for He was about to bring them into the land that He had promised to give them. He said to Joshua:

> I have given you every place where the sole of your foot treads, just as I promised Moses. Your territory will be from the wilderness and Lebanon to the great Euphrates River—all the land of the Hittites—and west to the Mediterranean Sea. No one will be able to stand against you as long as you live. I will be with you, just as I was with Moses. I will not leave you or forsake you (Joshua 1:3-5).

Being nervous before an event is normal. It tells us that what we're about to do is important. But God encourages us in the Bible to be brave and to take courage by performing for Him, the audience of One.

Don't allow those anxious feelings to keep you from challenging yourself. The outcome could surprise you! —*Jean Driscoll*

Go

1. Can you describe a time when you were anxious before a competition? Where was your focus? Were you able to overcome your anxiety?

2. What situations in competition typically make you anxious? If your approach to that situation were not anxious but courageous, on what would you be focusing?

3. Beyond sports, do you seek the Lord's strength to help you overcome little worries that plague your day?

Workout
Joshua 1:9; 2 Samuel 22:33;
Ephesians 3:20-21; Philippians 4:13

Overtime
God, help me to be calm and courageous during competition. Help me to focus on You, my audience of One. Amen.

Journal

Journal

28

The Gap

Ready

*I know, my God, that You test the heart and that
You are pleased with uprightness. I have willingly
given all these things with an upright heart,
and now I have seen Your people who are present
here giving joyfully and willingly to You.*

1 CHRONICLES 29:17

Set

The FCA Competitor's Creed (available at the back of this book) states: "My attitude on and off the field is above reproach—my conduct beyond criticism." This is a tough standard. Legendary Hall of Fame basketball coach John Wooden once said:

> A leader's most powerful ally is his or her own example. There is hypocrisy to the phrase "Do as I say, not as I do." I refused to make demands on my boys that I wasn't willing to live out in my own life.

As athletes and coaches, we too often desire to live a life that we know we have not committed in our hearts to living. We desire for our external life (the life that everyone sees—our wins and accomplishments) to be greater than our internal life (the life that no one sees—our thoughts and desires).

The best definition of hypocrisy I have heard is that it is the gap that exists between the public life and the private life. It's the difference between the external life and the internal life. God doesn't want there to be any gap at all. He wants every aspect of our lives to be filled with integrity.

As competitors, we face a constant war in our souls. We do not want others to see us as we really are. We are afraid that the gap will be exposed. However, God desires the exact opposite. He wants us to bring the dark things we have buried in our hearts into the light so that He can purify us.

Oswald Chambers wrote, "My worth to God in public is what I am in private." As a competitor for Christ, be committed to being real—to being gap free! —*Dan Britton*

Go

1. Where are the gaps in your life?

2. As a competitor, do you expect things from your teammates or peers that you are not willing to commit to yourself?

3. What does it mean to be a "real" competitor?

Workout

Psalms 25:21; 78:72; Proverbs 10:9;
Titus 2:6-8

Overtime

*Lord, I pray that You will reveal to me
any gaps in my life. I desire to live and
play for You as an authentic competitor.
It is by Your strength and power that those
gaps can be closed. Thank You for making
me complete by Your grace. Amen.*

Journal

Journal

29

Workout Partners

Ready

For I want very much to see you, that I may impart to you some spiritual gift to strengthen you, that is, to be mutually encouraged by each other's faith, both yours and mine.

ROMANS 1:11-12

Set

A workout partner is someone who will be there for you. It is a person who shares your desire to succeed and who is excited to train with you. It is someone who can't wait to be energized by your energy level.

In Paul's letter to the church in Rome, it is apparent that he couldn't wait to see the believers there and spend time with them. He was excited to help them train. He was excited to tell them about Jesus. He was excited to work with them and to be mutually encouraged by them.

We all need a workout partner who will help us in our spiritual training. We need someone who will make sure that we are reading our Bible each day. We need a partner who will commit to growing his or her own relationship with Jesus right alongside of us. We need someone who will support us when we are going through the rough stretches.

We all need someone who can encourage us and whom we can encourage. —*Michael Hill*

Go

1. Who is your athletic workout partner? Who is your spiritual workout partner? What similarities do you see in the ways that each of you trains?

2. How does your partner's attitude affect yours? What does that say about how your attitude likely affects him or her?

3. How can you take your spiritual workouts up a notch?

Workout

Proverbs 27:17; Ecclesiastes 4:9-12; Hebrews 3:13; 10:24-25; 1 John 1:3-4

Overtime

Father, let me find encouragement today from my Christian brothers and sisters. Let me be an encouragement to them as well. Use me to build Your Church. Bring me together with people who will help me grow my relationship with You. I thank You for fellowship, Father. In Jesus' name. Amen.

Two are better than one because they have a good reward for their efforts. For if either falls, his companion can lift him up; but pity the one who falls without another to lift him up (Ecclesiastes 4:9-10).

Journal

Journal

30

Team First

Ready

*Now may the God of endurance and
encouragement grant you agreement with one another,
according to Christ Jesus, so that you may glorify the
God and Father of our Lord Jesus Christ
with a united mind and voice.*

ROMANS 15:5-6

Set

I came to the Pittsburgh Steelers as a rookie in
1977. This was during their heyday—when they
were in the process of winning four Super
Bowls in six years. Looking at all the star players and future Hall of Fame guys they had on
their roster at the time, it was easy to think,
Well, that's why they're so good. But it really wasn't.

Once I got there, I saw how the team oper-
ated. It was the practices. It was everybody
working together. I think it's still possible to
achieve that kind of unity today. The good
teams have it. Even though you have star players, they understand that you can't just send 11
individuals out there and expect things to run
smoothly enough for you to win. The team's
success depends on how you practice, how you
work together, how you encourage one another,

and how you help a group of individuals become a unit. —*Tony Dungy*

Go

1. Can you think of some teams that had great talent but failed to succeed? What about some teams that had less talent but still achieved great things?

2. What do you think makes the difference between a team's success and its failure?

3. According to Romans 15:5-6, what are some of God's characteristics that can bring unity and team success? What should be the ultimate goal of any team?

Workout

John 17:21-23; Romans 14:19;
2 Corinthians 10:12

Overtime

Lord, grant me the endurance to work together with my teammates. Help me to encourage them in both the good and bad times so that we might glorify Your name. Amen.

Journal

Journal

31

For the Glory

Ready

No wise man, enchanter, magician or diviner
can explain to the king the mystery he has asked
about, but there is a God in heaven who reveals
mysteries. He has shown King Nebuchadnezzar
what will happen in days to come.

DANIEL 2:27-28, *NIV*

Set

As competitors, it is often difficult for us to give glory where glory is due. Training, discipline, perseverance and drive are all characteristics that can propel us to the next level, as we go from being good athletes to being great ones. Often after achieving a goal, we feel that it is our hard work that got us to that point. The praise, honor and glory are focused on us as individual athletes.

Daniel had a chance to take the glory for himself, but instead he chose to give it to the Lord. "No wise man, enchanter, magician or diviner can explain to the king the mystery he has asked about, but there is a God in heaven who reveals mysteries," he told the king (Daniel 2:27-28, *NIV*). "The great God has shown the king what will take place in the future. The dream is true and the interpretation is trustworthy" (Daniel 2:45, *NIV*).

The FCA Competitor's Creed states:

> I do not trust in myself.
> I do not boast in my abilities or believe in my own strength.
> I rely solely on the power of God.
> I compete for the pleasure of my Heavenly Father, the honor of Christ and the reputation of the Holy Spirit.

Our efforts must result in God's glory. To accept glory for ourselves is to rob God of His glory. —*Dan Britton*

Go

1. As an athlete, how much confidence do you have in your own abilities? Do you trust only in yourself?

2. What does it mean to compete for the pleasure of the heavenly Father?

3. If Daniel had scored a game's winning goal or received his team's MVP award, what do you think his response would have been?

Workout
2 Corinthians 5:1-10

Overtime

*Lord, it is difficult for me to give You all the glory.
Please forgive me for often taking credit when,
in reality, my athletic accomplishments should be
a fragrant offering to You. In my next competition,
help me to understand that my efforts must
result in Your glory. Amen.*

Journal

Journal

Shaun Alexander is a former NFL running back with the Seattle Seahawks and the Washington Redskins. He won the 2005 MVP award and was selected to three Pro Bowls.

Dan Britton serves as the FCA Executive Vice President of International Ministry and Training at FCA's National Support Center in Kansas City, Missouri. In high school and college, Dan was a standout lacrosse player. Dan and his family reside in Overland Park, Kansas.

Danny Burns is the director of Digital Ministry at FCA's National Support Center in Kansas City, Missouri. Danny helped lead the Northwest Missouri State Huddle as a varsity distance runner until 2004. He is one of the pastors at the Avenue Church and has a passion to see the gospel transform lives. He, his wife, Ashley, and his family reside in the Kansas City area.

Josh Carter is a teacher and head wrestling coach at Gibson City-Melvin-Sibley High School in Illinois. Josh is active in helping lead FCA in his school.

Tamika Catchings is a WNBA forward who plays for the Indiana Fever. She is a four-time WNBA Defensive Player of the Year, the league's

2011 MVP, and a two-time Olympic gold medalist. She is also the founder of the Catch the Stars Foundation, a mentoring program for young people in Indianapolis.

Fleceia Comeaux serves as the area director for the South Houston FCA office. She is a graduate of the University of Houston, where she played basketball and soccer for the Coogs.

Jean Driscoll won two Olympic silver medals and 12 Paralympic medals during her career as an elite wheelchair racer. Jean has won numerous prestigious awards and was recognized by *Sports Illustrated for Women* as one of the top 25 female athletes of the twentieth century.

Tony Dungy is the former head coach of the Indianapolis Colts, leading Indianapolis to victory in Super Bowl XLI. As a player, he was a member of the Pittsburgh Steelers team that won Super Bowl XIII. Tony currently works as a studio football analyst for NBC.

Steve Fitzhugh is the founder and executive director of PowerMoves, a national youth organization that uses the power of athletics, academics and the arts to help youth move into success and significance. Steve is also a national spokesperson for FCA's "One Way 2 Play—Drug Free!" program.

Harry Flaherty played professional football for the Philadelphia Eagles, Tampa Bay Bandits (USFL) and Dallas Cowboys. He was also a two-time AP All-America linebacker at Holy Cross. Harry has served as the New Jersey FCA state director since 1995. He resides in Oceanport, New Jersey, with his wife, Janine, four sons and one daughter.

Ryan Hall is an American long-distance runner who holds the U.S. record in the half marathon and was the first American to break the one-hour barrier. He holds the fastest marathon time among U.S.-born citizens and finished tenth at the 2008 Beijing Olympics.

Michael Hill is a former FCA staff member and coach. He lives and teaches in Haysville, Kansas. Michael has been blessed to have coached college and high school football and has spent years as a head cross-country coach at the high-school level. He and his wife, Andrea, have seven children, Jaycee, Avery, Chad, Tori, Amanda, Landen and Parker.

Elliot Johnson was a collegiate head coach for more than 25 years—8 of which he spent as the head baseball coach at Olivet Nazarene University. Coach Johnson's teams have won 11 conference, district or national titles and have appeared in 2 NAIA World Series.

Chris Klein is a former MLS midfielder with the Los Angeles Galaxy, Kansas City Wizards and Real Salt Lake. He won the MLS Cup with the Wizards in 2000 and has twice been named MLS Comeback Player of the Year.

Carl Miller played with the Dallas Cowboys under legendary coach Tom Landry. Carl speaks to many groups and is on staff with FCA in the Greater Fort Worth, Texas, area. He loves working with athletes of all ages and continues to encourage other professional athletes in their faith.

Kerry O'Neill is originally from Iowa and played basketball for Oral Roberts University in Tulsa, Oklahoma, and in 11 different countries. Kerry and his family make their home in Fredericksburg, Virginia, where Kerry serves as FCA director.

Joe Outlaw is a former collegiate football player and is currently a volunteer community baseball and football coach in the Atlanta area. Joe is the director of human resources with the North American Mission Board and also serves on the board of directors for the Metro Atlanta FCA.

Jimmy Page serves as a Vice President of Field Ministry for the Mid-Atlantic Region and is the National Director of the health and fitness ministry for FCA. Jimmy, his wife and four children live in Maryland.

Roxanne Robbins is the announcer and producer of "Faith Beyond the Game," a nationally syndicated radio program that airs weekly on SRN News. Roxanne was an official chaplain for athletes competing in the 1998 Winter Olympics in Nagano, Japan, and is a regular contributor to *Sports Spectrum* magazine.

Daniel Sepulveda is an NFL punter and was a member of the Super Bowl XLIII champion team. At Baylor University, he was a four-time All-Big 12 selection and three-time All-American, and he is the only college player to twice win the Ray Guy Award.

IMPACTING THE WORLD FOR CHRIST THROUGH SPORTS

FELLOWSHIP OF CHRISTIAN ATHLETES

Since 1954, the Fellowship of Christian Athletes has challenged athletes and coaches to impact the world for Jesus Christ. FCA is cultivating Christian principles in local communities nationwide by encouraging, equipping, and empowering others to serve as examples and make a difference. Reaching approximately 2 million people annually on the professional, college, high school, junior high and youth levels, FCA has grown into the largest sports ministry in the world. Through FCA's Four Cs of Ministry—coaches, campus, camps, and community—and the shared passion for athletics and faith, lives are changed for current and future generations.

FCA's Four Cs of Ministry

Coaches: Coaches are the heart of FCA. Our role is to minister to them by encouraging and equipping them to know and serve Christ. FCA ministeres to coaches through Bible studies, prayer support, discipleship and mentoring, resources, outreach events and retreats. FCA values coaches, first for who they are, and for what God has created them to do.

Campus: The Campus Ministry is initiated and led by student-athletes and coaches on junior high, high school and college campuses. The Campus Ministry types—Huddles, Team Bible Studies, Chaplain Programs and Coaches Bible Studies—are effective ways to establish FCA ministry presence, as well as outreach events such as One Way 2 Play-Drug Free programs, school assemblies and Fields of Faith.

Camp: Camp is a time of "inspiration and perspiration" for coaches and athletes to reach their potential by offering comprehensive athletic, spiritual and leadership training. FCA offers seven types of camps: Sports Camps, Leadership Camps, Coaches Camps, Power Camps, Partnership Camps, Team Camps and International Camps.

Community: FCA has ministries that reach the community through partnerships with local churches, businesses, parents and volunteers. These ministries not only reach out to the community, but also allow the community to invest in athletes and coaches. Non-school-based sports, adult ministries, youth sports, FCA Teams, clinics, resources and professional athlete ministries are the areas of Community Ministry.

Vision

To see the world impacted for Jesus Christ through the influence of coaches and athletes.

Mission

To present to coaches and athletes, and all whom they influence, the challenge and adventure of receiving Jesus Christ as Savior and Lord, serving Him in their relationships and in the fellowship of the Church.

Values

Integrity • Serving • Teamwork • Excellence

Fellowship of Christian Athletes
8701 Leeds Road • Kansas City, MO 64129
www.fca.org • fca@fca.org • 1-800-289-0909

COMPETITORS FOR CHRIST

FELLOWSHIP OF CHRISTIAN ATHLETES COMPETITOR'S CREED

I am a Christian first and last.
I am created in the likeness of God Almighty to bring Him glory.
I am a member of Team Jesus Christ.
I wear the colors of the cross.

I am a Competitor now and forever.
I am made to strive, to strain, to stretch and to succeed in the arena of competition.
I am a Christian Competitor and as such, I face my challenger with the face of Christ.

I do not trust in myself.
I do not boast in my abilities or believe in my own strength.
I rely solely on the power of God.
I compete for the pleasure of my Heavenly Father, the honor
of Christ and the reputation of the Holy Spirit.

My attitude on and off the field is above reproach—my conduct beyond criticism.
Whether I am preparing, practicing or playing,
I submit to God's authority and those He has put over me.
I respect my coaches, officials, teammates, and competitors out of respect for the Lord.

My body is the temple of Jesus Christ.
I protect it from within and without.
Nothing enters my body that does not honor the Living God.
My sweat is an offering to my Master. My soreness is a sacrifice to my Savior.

I give my all—all the time.
I do not give up. I do not give in. I do not give out.
I am the Lord's warrior—a competitor by conviction and a disciple of determination.
I am confident beyond reason because my confidence lies in Christ.
The results of my effort must result in His glory.

Let the competition begin.
Let the glory be God's.

Sign the Creed • Go to www.fca.org
© 2012 FCA

FELLOWSHIP OF CHRISTIAN ATHLETES COACH'S MANDATE

Pray as though nothing of eternal value is going
to happen in my athletes' lives unless God does it.

Prepare each practice and game as giving "my utmost for His highest."

Seek not to be served by my athletes for personal gain, but seek
to serve them as Christ served the church.

Be satisfied not with producing a good record, but with producing good athletes.

Attend carefully to my private and public walk with God, knowing that the
athlete will never rise to a standard higher than that being lived by the coach.

Exalt Christ in my coaching, trusting the Lord will then draw athletes to Himself.

Desire to have a growing hunger for God's Word, for personal
obedience, for fruit of the spirit and for saltiness in competition.

Depend solely upon God for transformation—one athlete at a time.

Preach Christ's word in a Christ-like demeanor, on and off the field of competition.

Recognize that it is impossible to bring glory to both myself
and Christ at the same time.

Allow my coaching to exude the fruit of the Spirit,
thus producing Christ-like athletes.

Trust God to produce in my athletes His chosen purposes,
regardless of whether the wins are readily visible.

Coach with humble gratitude, as one privileged to be God's coach.